FIRST 50 SONGS
YOU SHOULD PLAY ON THE TROMBONE

ISBN 978-1-5400-0432-1

7777 W. BLUEMOUND RD. P.O. BOX 13819 MILWAUKEE, WI 53213

Visit Hal Leonard Online at
www.halleonard.com

ALL OF ME

TROMBONE

Words and Music by JOHN STEPHENS
and TOBY GAD

Slowly, in 2

1.
1st time D.C.
2nd time Fine

2.

D.S. al Fine
(take 1st ending)

ALL YOU NEED IS LOVE

TROMBONE

Words and Music by JOHN LENNON
and PAUL McCARTNEY

AMAZING GRACE

TROMBONE

Traditional American Melody

BASIN STREET BLUES

TROMBONE

Words and Music by
SPENCER WILLIAMS

BEST SONG EVER

TROMBONE

Words and Music by EDWARD DREWETT,
WAYNE HECTOR, JULIAN BUNETTA
and JOHN RYAN

CARNIVAL OF VENICE

TROMBONE

By JULIUS BENEDICT

Moderately, with motion

CIRCLE OF LIFE

from THE LION KING

TROMBONE

Music by ELTON JOHN
Lyrics by TIM RICE

EVERMORE

from BEAUTY AND THE BEAST

TROMBONE

Music by ALAN MENKEN
Lyrics by TIM RICE

FLY ME TO THE MOON
(In Other Words)

TROMBONE

Words and Music by
BART HOWARD

FIGHT SONG

TROMBONE

Words and Music by RACHEL PLATTEN
and DAVE BASSETT

THE FOOL ON THE HILL

Words and Music by JOHN LENNON
and PAUL McCARTNEY

TROMBONE

Slowly

GOD BLESS AMERICA®

TROMBONE

Words and Music by
IRVING BERLIN

THE GODFATHER
(Love Theme)
from the Paramount Picture THE GODFATHER

TROMBONE

By NINO ROTA

Slowly and expressively

GOODBYE

TROMBONE

Words and Music by
GORDON JENKINS

HALLELUJAH

TROMBONE

Words and Music by
LEONARD COHEN

HAPPY

from DESPICABLE ME 2

TROMBONE

Words and Music by
PHARRELL WILLIAMS

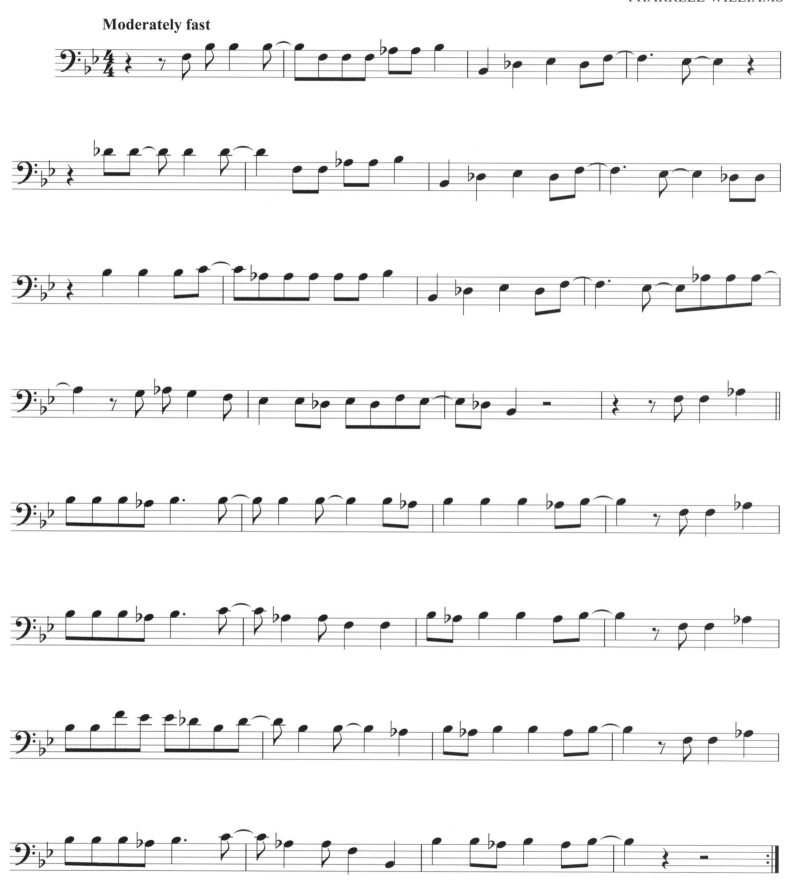

HELLO

TROMBONE

Words and Music by
LIONEL RICHIE

Slow Ballad

HELLO, DOLLY!

from HELLO, DOLLY!

TROMBONE

Music and Lyric by
JERRY HERMAN

HONEYSUCKLE ROSE
from AIN'T MISBEHAVIN'

TROMBONE

Words by ANDY RAZAF
Music by THOMAS "FATS" WALLER

HOW DEEP IS YOUR LOVE
from the Motion Picture SATURDAY NIGHT FEVER

TROMBONE

Words and Music by BARRY GIBB,
ROBIN GIBB and MAURICE GIBB

THE HUSTLE

TROMBONE

Words and Music by
VAN McCOY

I WILL ALWAYS LOVE YOU

TROMBONE

Words and Music by
DOLLY PARTON

small notes optional

I'M GETTING SENTIMENTAL OVER YOU

TROMBONE

Words by NED WASHINGTON
Music by GEORGE BASSMAN

MARIE

TROMBONE

Words and Music by
IRVING BERLIN

JUST GIVE ME A REASON

TROMBONE

Words and Music by ALECIA MOORE,
JEFF BHASKER and NATE RUESS

29

CODA

JUST THE WAY YOU ARE

TROMBONE

Words and Music by BRUNO MARS,
ARI LEVINE, PHILIP LAWRENCE,
KHARI CAIN and KHALIL WALTON

Moderately

LET IT GO
from FROZEN

TROMBONE

Music and Lyrics by KRISTEN ANDERSON-LOPEZ
and ROBERT LOPEZ

Slowly, in 2

Fine

D.S. al Fine

MAS QUE NADA

TROMBONE

Words and Music by
JORGE BEN

MISSION: IMPOSSIBLE THEME

From the Paramount Television Series MISSION: IMPOSSIBLE

TROMBONE

By LALO SCHIFRIN

MY HEART WILL GO ON
(Love Theme from 'Titanic')
from the Paramount and Twentieth Century Fox Motion Picture TITANIC

TROMBONE

Music by JAMES HORNER
Lyric by WILL JENNINGS

OLD TIME ROCK & ROLL

TROMBONE

Words and Music by GEORGE JACKSON
and THOMAS E. JONES III

(small notes optional)

NIGHT TRAIN

TROMBONE

Words by OSCAR WASHINGTON
and LEWIS C. SIMPKINS
Music by JIMMY FORREST

OPUS ONE

TROMBONE

Words and Music by
SY OLIVER

PETER GUNN
Theme Song from the Television Series

TROMBONE

By HENRY MANCINI

THE PINK PANTHER

from THE PINK PANTHER

TROMBONE

By HENRY MANCINI

PURE IMAGINATION
from WILLY WONKA AND THE CHOCOLATE FACTORY

TROMBONE

Words and Music by LESLIE BRICUSSE
and ANTHONY NEWLEY

ROAR

TROMBONE

Words and Music by KATY PERRY,
MAX MARTIN, DR. LUKE,
BONNIE McKEE and HENRY WALTER

Moderately

ROLLING IN THE DEEP

TROMBONE

Words and Music by ADELE ADKINS
and PAUL EPWORTH

SATIN DOLL

TROMBONE

By DUKE ELLINGTON

SEVENTY SIX TROMBONES

from Meredith Willson's THE MUSIC MAN

TROMBONE

By MEREDITH WILLSON

March tempo

SEE YOU AGAIN

from FURIOUS 7

TROMBONE

Words and Music by CAMERON THOMAZ,
CHARLIE PUTH, JUSTIN FRANKS
and ANDREW CEDAR

SHAKE IT OFF

TROMBONE

Words and Music by TAYLOR SWIFT,
MAX MARTIN and SHELLBACK

STAND BY ME

Words and Music by JERRY LEIBER,
MIKE STOLLER and BEN E. KING

TROMBONE

Moderately, with a beat

THE STAR-SPANGLED BANNER

TROMBONE

Words by FRANCIS SCOTT KEY
Music by JOHN STAFFORD SMITH

STAY WITH ME

TROMBONE

Words and Music by SAM SMITH,
JAMES NAPIER, WILLIAM EDWARD PHILLIPS,
TOM PETTY and JEFF LYNNE

STOMPIN' AT THE SAVOY

TROMBONE

By BENNY GOODMAN,
EDGAR SAMPSON and CHICK WEBB

Bright Swing

SUMMERTIME
from PORGY AND BESS®

TROMBONE

Music and Lyrics by GEORGE GERSHWIN,
DuBOSE and DOROTHY HEYWARD
and IRA GERSHWIN

TEQUILA

TROMBONE

By CHUCK RIO

UPTOWN FUNK

TROMBONE

Words and Music by MARK RONSON,
BRUNO MARS, PHILIP LAWRENCE, JEFF BHASKER, DEVON GALLASPY,
NICHOLAUS WILLIAMS, LONNIE SIMMONS, RONNIE WILSON,
CHARLES WILSON, RUDOLPH TAYLOR and ROBERT WILSON

A TASTE OF HONEY

TROMBONE

Words by RIC MARLOW
Music by BOBBY SCOTT

HAL·LEONARD INSTRUMENTAL PLAY-ALONG

Your favorite songs are arranged just for solo instrumentalists with this outstanding series. Each book includes great full-accompaniment play-along audio so you can sound just like a pro!

Check out **halleonard.com** for songlists and more titles!

12 Pop Hits
12 songs
00261790	Flute	00261795	Horn
00261791	Clarinet	00261796	Trombone
00261792	Alto Sax	00261797	Violin
00261793	Tenor Sax	00261798	Viola
00261794	Trumpet	00261799	Cello

The Very Best of Bach
15 selections
00225371	Flute	00225376	Horn
00225372	Clarinet	00225377	Trombone
00225373	Alto Sax	00225378	Violin
00225374	Tenor Sax	00225379	Viola
00225375	Trumpet	00225380	Cello

The Beatles
15 songs
00225330	Flute	00225335	Horn
00225331	Clarinet	00225336	Trombone
00225332	Alto Sax	00225337	Violin
00225333	Tenor Sax	00225338	Viola
00225334	Trumpet	00225339	Cello

Chart Hits
12 songs
00146207	Flute	00146212	Horn
00146208	Clarinet	00146213	Trombone
00146209	Alto Sax	00146214	Violin
00146210	Tenor Sax	00146211	Trumpet
00146216	Cello		

Christmas Songs
12 songs
00146855	Flute	00146863	Horn
00146858	Clarinet	00146864	Trombone
00146859	Alto Sax	00146866	Violin
00146860	Tenor Sax	00146867	Viola
00146862	Trumpet	00146868	Cello

Contemporary Broadway
15 songs
00298704	Flute	00298709	Horn
00298705	Clarinet	00298710	Trombone
00298706	Alto Sax	00298711	Violin
00298707	Tenor Sax	00298712	Viola
00298708	Trumpet	00298713	Cello

Disney Movie Hits
12 songs
00841420	Flute	00841424	Horn
00841687	Oboe	00841425	Trombone
00841421	Clarinet	00841426	Violin
00841422	Alto Sax	00841427	Viola
00841686	Tenor Sax	00841428	Cello
00841423	Trumpet		

Prices, contents, and availability subject to change without notice.

Disney characters and artwork ™ & © 2021 Disney

Disney Solos
12 songs
00841404	Flute	00841506	Oboe
00841406	Alto Sax	00841409	Trumpet
00841407	Horn	00841410	Violin
00841411	Viola	00841412	Cello
00841405	Clarinet/Tenor Sax		
00841408	Trombone/Baritone		
00841553	Mallet Percussion		

Dixieland Favorites
15 songs
00268756	Flute	0068759	Trumpet
00268757	Clarinet	00268760	Trombone
00268758	Alto Sax		

Billie Eilish
9 songs
00345648	Flute	00345653	Horn
00345649	Clarinet	00345654	Trombone
00345650	Alto Sax	00345655	Violin
00345651	Tenor Sax	00345656	Viola
00345652	Trumpet	00345657	Cello

Favorite Movie Themes
13 songs
00841166	Flute	00841168	Trumpet
00841167	Clarinet	00841170	Trombone
00841169	Alto Sax	00841296	Violin

Gospel Hymns
15 songs
00194648	Flute	00194654	Trombone
00194649	Clarinet	00194655	Violin
00194650	Alto Sax	00194656	Viola
00194651	Tenor Sax	00194657	Cello
00194652	Trumpet		

Great Classical Themes
15 songs
00292727	Flute	00292733	Horn
00292728	Clarinet	00292735	Trombone
00292729	Alto Sax	00292736	Violin
00292730	Tenor Sax	00292737	Viola
00292732	Trumpet	00292738	Cello

The Greatest Showman
8 songs
00277389	Flute	00277394	Horn
00277390	Clarinet	00277395	Trombone
00277391	Alto Sax	00277396	Violin
00277392	Tenor Sax	00277397	Viola
00277393	Trumpet	00277398	Cello

Irish Favorites
31 songs
00842489	Flute	00842495	Trombone
00842490	Clarinet	00842496	Violin
00842491	Alto Sax	00842497	Viola
00842493	Trumpet	00842498	Cello
00842494	Horn		

Michael Jackson
11 songs
00119495	Flute	00119499	Trumpet
00119496	Clarinet	00119501	Trombone
00119497	Alto Sax	00119503	Violin
00119498	Tenor Sax	00119502	Accomp.

Jazz & Blues
14 songs
00841438	Flute	00841441	Trumpet
00841439	Clarinet	00841443	Trombone
00841440	Alto Sax	00841444	Violin
00841442	Tenor Sax		

Jazz Classics
12 songs
00151812	Flute	00151816	Trumpet
00151813	Clarinet	00151818	Trombone
00151814	Alto Sax	00151819	Violin
00151815	Tenor Sax	00151821	Cello

Les Misérables
13 songs
00842292	Flute	00842297	Horn
00842293	Clarinet	00842298	Trombone
00842294	Alto Sax	00842299	Violin
00842295	Tenor Sax	00842300	Viola
00842296	Trumpet	00842301	Cello

Metallica
12 songs
02501327	Flute	02502454	Horn
02501339	Clarinet	02501329	Trombone
02501332	Alto Sax	02501334	Violin
02501333	Tenor Sax	02501335	Viola
02501330	Trumpet	02501338	Cello

Motown Classics
15 songs
00842572	Flute	00842576	Trumpet
00842573	Clarinet	00842578	Trombone
00842574	Alto Sax	00842579	Violin
00842575	Tenor Sax		

Pirates of the Caribbean
16 songs
00842183	Flute	00842188	Horn
00842184	Clarinet	00842189	Trombone
00842185	Alto Sax	00842190	Violin
00842186	Tenor Sax	00842191	Viola
00842187	Trumpet	00842192	Cello

Queen
17 songs
00285402	Flute	00285407	Horn
00285403	Clarinet	00285408	Trombone
00285404	Alto Sax	00285409	Violin
00285405	Tenor Sax	00285410	Viola
00285406	Trumpet	00285411	Cello

Simple Songs
14 songs
00249081	Flute	00249087	Horn
00249093	Oboe	00249089	Trombone
00249082	Clarinet	00249090	Violin
00249083	Alto Sax	00249091	Viola
00249084	Tenor Sax	00249092	Cello
00249086	Trumpet	00249094	Mallets

Superhero Themes
14 songs
00363195	Flute	00363200	Horn
00363196	Clarinet	00363201	Trombone
00363197	Alto Sax	00363202	Violin
00363198	Tenor Sax	00363203	Viola
00363199	Trumpet	00363204	Cello

Star Wars
16 songs
00350900	Flute	00350907	Horn
00350913	Oboe	00350908	Trombone
00350903	Clarinet	00350909	Violin
00350904	Alto Sax	00350910	Viola
00350905	Tenor Sax	00350911	Cello
00350906	Trumpet	00350914	Mallet

Taylor Swift
15 songs
00842532	Flute	00842537	Horn
00842533	Clarinet	00842538	Trombone
00842534	Alto Sax	00842539	Violin
00842535	Tenor Sax	00842540	Viola
00842536	Trumpet	00842541	Cello

Video Game Music
13 songs
00283877	Flute	00283883	Horn
00283878	Clarinet	00283884	Trombone
00283879	Alto Sax	00283885	Violin
00283880	Tenor Sax	00283886	Viola
00283882	Trumpet	00283887	Cello

Wicked
13 songs
00842236	Flute	00842241	Horn
00842237	Clarinet	00842242	Trombone
00842238	Alto Sax	00842243	Violin
00842239	Tenor Sax	00842244	Viola
00842240	Trumpet	00842245	Cello

HAL·LEONARD®

101 SONGS

BIG COLLECTIONS OF FAVORITE SONGS ARRANGED FOR SOLO INSTRUMENTALISTS.

101 BROADWAY SONGS

00154199	Flute	$15.99
00154200	Clarinet	$15.99
00154201	Alto Sax	$15.99
00154202	Tenor Sax	$16.99
00154203	Trumpet	$15.99
00154204	Horn	$15.99
00154205	Trombone	$15.99
00154206	Violin	$15.99

00154207 Viola.................................$15.99
00154208 Cello.................................$15.99

101 DISNEY SONGS

00244104	Flute	$17.99
00244106	Clarinet	$17.99
00244107	Alto Sax	$17.99
00244108	Tenor Sax	$17.99
00244109	Trumpet	$17.99
00244112	Horn	$17.99
00244120	Trombone	$17.99
00244121	Violin	$17.99

00244125 Viola.................................$17.99
00244126 Cello.................................$17.99

101 MOVIE HITS

00158087	Flute	$15.99
00158088	Clarinet	$15.99
00158089	Alto Sax	$15.99
00158090	Tenor Sax	$15.99
00158091	Trumpet	$15.99
00158092	Horn	$15.99
00158093	Trombone	$15.99
00158094	Violin	$15.99

00158095 Viola.................................$15.99
00158096 Cello.................................$15.99

101 CHRISTMAS SONGS

00278637	Flute	$15.99
00278638	Clarinet	$15.99
00278639	Alto Sax	$15.99
00278640	Tenor Sax	$15.99
00278641	Trumpet	$15.99
00278642	Horn	$14.99
00278643	Trombone	$15.99
00278644	Violin	$15.99

00278645 Viola.................................$15.99
00278646 Cello.................................$15.99

101 HIT SONGS

00194561	Flute	$17.99
00197182	Clarinet	$17.99
00197183	Alto Sax	$17.99
00197184	Tenor Sax	$17.99
00197185	Trumpet	$17.99
00197186	Horn	$17.99
00197187	Trombone	$17.99
00197188	Violin	$17.99

00197189 Viola.................................$17.99
00197190 Cello.................................$17.99

101 POPULAR SONGS

00224722	Flute	$17.99
00224723	Clarinet	$17.99
00224724	Alto Sax	$17.99
00224725	Tenor Sax	$17.99
00224726	Trumpet	$17.99
00224727	Horn	$17.99
00224728	Trombone	$17.99
00224729	Violin	$17.99

00224730 Viola.................................$17.99
00224731 Cello.................................$17.99

101 CLASSICAL THEMES

00155315	Flute	$15.99
00155317	Clarinet	$15.99
00155318	Alto Sax	$15.99
00155319	Tenor Sax	$15.99
00155320	Trumpet	$15.99
00155321	Horn	$15.99
00155322	Trombone	$15.99
00155323	Violin	$15.99

00155324 Viola.................................$15.99
00155325 Cello.................................$15.99

101 JAZZ SONGS

00146363	Flute	$15.99
00146364	Clarinet	$15.99
00146366	Alto Sax	$15.99
00146367	Tenor Sax	$15.99
00146368	Trumpet	$15.99
00146369	Horn	$14.99
00146370	Trombone	$15.99
00146371	Violin	$15.99

00146372 Viola.................................$15.99
00146373 Cello.................................$15.99

101 MOST BEAUTIFUL SONGS

00291023	Flute	$16.99
00291041	Clarinet	$16.99
00291042	Alto Sax	$17.99
00291043	Tenor Sax	$17.99
00291044	Trumpet	$16.99
00291045	Horn	$16.99
00291046	Trombone	$16.99
00291047	Violin	$16.99

00291048 Viola.................................$16.99
00291049 Cello.................................$17.99

See complete song lists and sample pages at www.halleonard.com

HAL•LEONARD®
www.halleonard.com

Prices, contents and availability subject to change without notice.

ARTIST TRANSCRIPTIONS®

Artist Transcriptions are authentic, note-for-note transcriptions of today's hottest artists in jazz, pop and rock. These outstanding, accurate arrangements are in an easy-to-read format which includes all essential lines. **Artist Transcriptions** can be used to perform, sequence or for reference.

FLUTE
00672379	Eric Dolphy Collection	$19.95
00672582	The Very Best of James Galway	$19.99
00672372	James Moody Collection – Sax and Flute	$19.95

GUITAR & BASS
00660113	Guitar Style of George Benson	$19.99
00672573	Ray Brown – Legendary Jazz Bassist	$22.99
00672331	Ron Carter Collection	$24.99
00660115	Al Di Meola – Friday Night in San Francisco	$24.99
00125617	Best of Herb Ellis	$19.99
00699306	Jim Hall – Exploring Jazz Guitar	$19.99
00672353	The Joe Pass Collection	$22.99
00673216	John Patitucci	$22.99
00672374	Johnny Smith – Guitar Solos	$24.99

PIANO & KEYBOARD
00672487	Monty Alexander Plays Standards	$19.95
00672520	Count Basie Collection	$19.95
00192307	Bebop Piano Legends	$19.99
00113680	Blues Piano Legends	$22.99
00672526	The Bill Charlap Collection	$19.99
00278003	A Charlie Brown Christmas	$19.99
00672300	Chick Corea – Paint the World	$19.99
00146105	Bill Evans – Alone	$21.99
00672548	The Mastery of Bill Evans	$16.99
00672365	Bill Evans – Play Standards	$22.99
00121885	Bill Evans – Time Remembered	$22.99
00672510	Bill Evans Trio Vol. 1: 1959-1961	$29.99
00672511	Bill Evans Trio Vol. 2: 1962-1965	$27.99
00672512	Bill Evans Trio Vol. 3: 1968-1974	$29.99
00672513	Bill Evans Trio Vol. 4: 1979-1980	$24.95
00193332	Erroll Garner – Concert by the Sea	$22.99
00672486	Vince Guaraldi Collection	$19.99
00289644	The Definitive Vince Guaraldi	$39.99
00672419	Herbie Hancock Collection	$22.99
00672438	Hampton Hawes Collection	$19.95
00672322	Ahmad Jamal Collection	$27.99
00255671	Jazz Piano Masterpieces	$22.99
00124367	Jazz Piano Masters Play Rodgers & Hammerstein	$19.99
00672564	Best of Jeff Lorber	$19.99

00672476	Brad Mehldau Collection	$24.99
00672388	Best of Thelonious Monk	$22.99
00672389	Thelonious Monk Collection	$24.99
00672390	Thelonious Monk Plays Jazz Standards – Volume 1	$24.99
00672391	Thelonious Monk Plays Jazz Standards – Volume 2	$24.99
00672433	Jelly Roll Morton – The Piano Rolls	$19.99
00264094	Oscar Peterson – Night Train	$19.99
00672544	Oscar Peterson – Originals	$15.99
00672531	Oscar Peterson – Plays Duke Ellington	$27.99
00672563	Oscar Peterson – A Royal Wedding Suite	$19.99
00672569	Oscar Peterson – Tracks	$19.99
00672533	Oscar Peterson – Trios	$39.99
00672534	Very Best of Oscar Peterson	$27.99
00672371	Bud Powell Classics	$22.99
00672376	Bud Powell Collection	$24.99
00672507	Gonzalo Rubalcaba Collection	$19.95
00672303	Horace Silver Collection	$24.99
00672316	Art Tatum Collection	$27.99
00672355	Art Tatum Solo Book	$22.99
00672357	The Billy Taylor Collection	$24.95
00673215	McCoy Tyner	$22.99
00672321	Cedar Walton Collection	$19.95
00672519	Kenny Werner Collection	$19.95

SAXOPHONE
00672566	The Mindi Abair Collection	$14.99
00673244	Julian "Cannonball" Adderley Collection	$22.99
00673237	Michael Brecker	$24.99
00672429	Michael Brecker Collection	$24.99
00672529	John Coltrane – Giant Steps	$22.99
00672494	John Coltrane – A Love Supreme	$17.99
00672493	John Coltrane Plays "Coltrane Changes"	$19.95
00672453	John Coltrane Plays Standards	$24.99
00673233	John Coltrane Solos	$29.99
00672328	Paul Desmond Collection	$22.99
00672530	Kenny Garrett Collection	$24.99
00699375	Stan Getz	$19.99
00672377	Stan Getz – Bossa Novas	$24.99
00673254	Great Tenor Sax Solos	$22.99

00672523	Coleman Hawkins Collection	$24.99
00672330	Best of Joe Henderson	$24.99
00673239	Best of Kenny G	$22.99
00673229	Kenny G – Breathless	$19.99
00672462	Kenny G – Classics in the Key of G	$24.99
00672485	Kenny G – Faith: A Holiday Album	$17.99
00672373	Kenny G – The Moment	$22.99
00672498	Jackie McLean Collection	$19.95
00672372	James Moody Collection – Sax and Flute	$19.95
00672539	Gerry Mulligan Collection	$24.99
00102751	Sonny Rollins, Art Blakey & Kenny Drew with the Modern Jazz Quartet	$17.99
00675000	David Sanborn Collection	$19.99
00672491	The New Best of Wayne Shorter	$24.99
00672550	The Sonny Stitt Collection	$19.95
00672524	Lester Young Collection	$22.99

TROMBONE
00672332	J.J. Johnson Collection	$24.99
00672489	Steve Turré Collection	$19.99

TRUMPET
00672557	Herb Alpert Collection	$19.99
00672480	Louis Armstrong Collection	$19.99
00672481	Louis Armstrong Plays Standards	$19.99
00672435	Chet Baker Collection	$24.99
00672556	Best of Chris Botti	$19.99
00672448	Miles Davis – Originals, Vol. 1	$19.99
00672451	Miles Davis – Originals, Vol. 2	$19.95
00672449	Miles Davis – Standards, Vol. 2	$19.95
00672479	Dizzy Gillespie Collection	$19.95
00673214	Freddie Hubbard	$19.99
00672506	Chuck Mangione Collection	$22.99
00672525	Arturo Sandoval – Trumpet Evolution	$19.99

HAL•LEONARD®

Visit our web site for songlists or to order online from your favorite music retailer at
www.halleonard.com

Prices, content, and availability subject to change without notice.

The Best-Selling Jazz Book of All Time Is Now Legal!

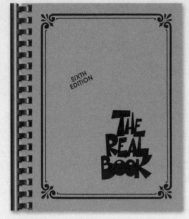

The Real Books are the most popular jazz books of all time. Since the 1970s, musicians have trusted these volumes to get them through every gig, night after night. The problem is that the books were illegally produced and distributed, without any regard to copyright law, or royalties paid to the composers who created these musical masterpieces.

Hal Leonard is very proud to present the first legitimate and legal editions of these books ever produced. You won't even notice the difference, other than all the notorious errors being fixed: the covers and typeface look the same, the song lists are nearly identical, and the price for our edition is even cheaper than the originals!

Every conscientious musician will appreciate that these books are now produced accurately and ethically, benefitting the songwriters that we owe for some of the greatest tunes of all time!

VOLUME 1
00240221	C Edition	$49.99
00240224	B♭ Edition	$49.99
00240225	E♭ Edition	$49.99
00240226	Bass Clef Edition	$49.99
00286389	F Edition	$39.99
00240292	C Edition 6 x 9	$39.99
00240339	B♭ Edition 6 x 9	$44.99
00147792	Bass Clef Edition 6 x 9	$39.99
00200984	Online Backing Tracks: Selections	$45.00
00110604	Book/USB Flash Drive Backing Tracks Pack	$85.00
00110599	USB Flash Drive Only	$50.00

VOLUME 2
00240222	C Edition	$49.99
00240227	B♭ Edition	$49.99
00240228	E♭ Edition	$49.99
00240229	Bass Clef Edition	$49.99
00240293	C Edition 6 x 9	$39.99
00125900	B♭ Edition 6 x 9	$39.99
00125900	The Real Book – Mini Edition	$39.99
00204126	Backing Tracks on USB Flash Drive	$55.00
00204131	C Edition – USB Flash Drive Pack	$85.00

VOLUME 3
00240233	C Edition	$49.99
00240284	B♭ Edition	$49.99
00240285	E♭ Edition	$49.99
00240286	Bass Clef Edition	$49.99
00240338	C Edition 6 x 9	$39.99

VOLUME 4
00240296	C Edition	$49.99
00103348	B♭ Edition	$49.99
00103349	E♭ Edition	$49.99
00103350	Bass Clef Edition	$49.99

VOLUME 5
00240349	C Edition	$49.99
00175278	B♭ Edition	$49.99
00175279	E♭ Edition	$49.99

VOLUME 6
00240534	C Edition	$49.99
00223637	E♭ Edition	$49.99

Also available:
00154230	The Real Bebop Book C Edition	$34.99
00295069	The Real Bebop Book E♭ Edition	$34.99
00295068	The Real Bebop Book B♭ Edition	$34.99
00240264	The Real Blues Book	$39.99
00310910	The Real Bluegrass Book	$39.99
00240223	The Real Broadway Book	$39.99
00240440	The Trane Book	$25.00
00125426	The Real Country Book	$45.00
00269721	The Real Miles Davis Book C Edition	$29.99
00269723	The Real Miles Davis Book B♭ Edition	$29.99
00240355	The Real Dixieland Book C Edition	$39.99
00294853	The Real Dixieland Book E♭ Edition	$39.99
00122335	The Real Dixieland Book B♭ Edition	$39.99
00240235	The Duke Ellington Real Book	$29.99
00240268	The Real Jazz Solos Book	$44.99
00240348	The Real Latin Book C Edition	$39.99
00127107	The Real Latin Book B♭ Edition	$39.99
00120809	The Pat Metheny Real Book C Edition	$34.99
00252119	The Pat Metheny Real Book B♭ Edition	$29.99
00240358	The Charlie Parker Real Book C Edition	$25.00
00275997	The Charlie Parker Real Book E♭ Edition	$25.00
00118324	The Real Pop Book C Edition – Vol. 1	$45.00
00295066	The Real Pop Book B♭ Edition – Vol. 1	$39.99
00286451	The Real Pop Book C Edition – Vol. 2	$45.00
00240331	The Bud Powell Real Book	$25.00
00240437	The Real R&B Book C Edition	$45.00
00276590	The Real R&B Book B♭ Edition	$45.00
00240313	The Real Rock Book	$39.99
00240323	The Real Rock Book – Vol. 2	$39.99
00240359	The Real Tab Book	$39.99
00240317	The Real Worship Book	$35.00

THE REAL CHRISTMAS BOOK
00240306	C Edition	$39.99
00240345	B♭ Edition	$35.00
00240346	E♭ Edition	$35.00
00240347	Bass Clef Edition	$35.00

THE REAL VOCAL BOOK
00240230	Volume 1 High Voice	$40.00
00240307	Volume 1 Low Voice	$40.00
00240231	Volume 2 High Voice	$39.99
00240308	Volume 2 Low Voice	$39.99
00240391	Volume 3 High Voice	$39.99
00240392	Volume 3 Low Voice	$39.99
00118318	Volume 4 High Voice	$39.99
00118319	Volume 4 Low Voice	$39.99

Complete song lists online at www.halleonard.com

Prices, content, and availability subject to change without notice.